ELASTIC

OTHER TITLES FROM THE EMMA PRESS

POETRY PAMPHLETS

Dragonish, by Emma Simon
Pisanki, by Zosia Kuczyńska
Who Seemed Alive & Altogether Real, by Padraig Regan
Paisley, by Rakhshan Rizwan

SHORT STORIES

First fox, by Leanne Radojkovich
Postcard Stories, by Jan Carson
The Secret Box, by Daina Tabūna
Once Upon A Time In Birmingham, by Louise Palfreyman

POETRY ANTHOLOGIES

The Emma Press Anthology of Love
Some Cannot Be Caught: The Emma Press Book of Beasts
In Transit: Poems of Travel
Second Place Rosette: Poems about Britain
Everything That Can Happen: Poems about the Future

BOOKS FOR CHILDREN

The Book of Clouds, by Juris Kronbergs
Everyone's the Smartest, by Contra
The Dog Who Found Sorrow, by Rūta Briede
The Head that Wears a Crown: Poems about Kings and Queens

POETRY AND ART SQUARES

If I Lay on my Back I Saw Nothing but Naked Women,
by Jacqueline Saphra, illustrated by Mark Andrew Owen
AWOL, by John Fuller and Andrew Wynn Owen,
illustrated by Emma Wright
Now You Can Look, by Julia Bird, illustrated by Anna Vaivare

ELASTIC GLUE

By Kathy Pimlott

THE EMMA PRESS

For Ella and Eliza

and for the Gardeners and the gardener

THE EMMA PRESS

First published in the UK in 2019 by the Emma Press Ltd

ISBN 978-1-912915-07-1

A CIP catalogue record of this book
is available from the British Library.

Printed and bound in the UK
by Impact Print & Design, Hereford.

The Emma Press
theemmapress.com
hello@theemmapress.com
Birmingham, UK

CONTENTS

They count on you getting tired, giving up

No-one lives here, you'd think, in the city's glitzy heart
except the agile young wanting to shimmy and shine
before taking a van out to somewhere more... private.

Yet here we are, in infill blocks we made them build
all those years ago, knowing your mum, your kids
since before they had their own, so close we hear

each other's sneezes, dying. Upstairs, temporary men
keep Spanish hours that clatter on their wooden floor,
my bedroom ceiling. They'll go. I know who plays away,

who cooks mackerel, who's been inside, uses Economy 7,
tunes in to Magic Radio. I know we're on borrowed time.
Where are the old girls of the market, theatres, print?

Gone to Guinnesses in the sky. Money wants no-one
to belong here, just pass through, hold no memories
worth fighting for to temper plans to squeeze the streets,

trick them out in shoddy to look like style, smell like profit.
Silly us. All that time we thought it ours, rallied, witnessed,
held the line, all that grief, just making it nice for Money.

Seven Dials: The Rookery Redux

The rain collects by drains stopped up
with fatbergs from the eateries,
in cracks and trips of paving stones
and setts lifted and re-laid. Step carelessly

and soak your shoes. Do you belong here?
Do you loop grey nets to foil
the suck and growl of traffic's heat?
Do you open your windows at all?

At night the seven streets pinball
each drunk chorus, each deal undone,
each spat. Roused sleepers turn
and mutter vows to flee to Harpenden,

Peterborough, somewhere normal.
Money's what it's always been about,
this star conceived for profit,
more rental by the frontage foot

than that for squares. Cute schemes
leap and crash, leave logos,
hidden eglomise, blind windows.
The crack mob keeps its ground, Soho

to St Giles, between cameras and lights.
Watchful, loose-jointed, urgent,
heads over cupped palms,
with sudden limping dashes they feint,

twist and turn, wry faced and pissen pants,
hopeless and eternally hunting
for that one good deal among the pop-ups,
the fairy-lit trees, the bunting.

Site of Special Scientific Interest

The island has been left to dormice, foxes, hives
and the water plant. An old Peace sprawls,
flushing yellow to pink. The rest has gone over.
Across the bridge it's biblical: plagues lay waste
to fruit and crucifers and just when you thought
you'd escaped, a wet spell incubates late blight.

Mice spoil apples, roll spent whisky bottles
across shed floors. Enthusiasms flare
then gutter, pricey secateurs are left
among the raspberry canes and drums
of half-steeped comfrey sludge reek brown.
Each season brings new immolations, strokes.

Someone broke into Reg's shed, made off
with a strimmer, several tins of soup. I think
of them gingerly tilting their bowls. In the event
of a Complete Breakdown we'll almost certainly
get a gun. Chicken Jim has one, thinks he's the boss
but he no longer has chickens, foxes got them all.

Borlotti always do well, their wine-freckled beans
the eggs of a very small bird. There's talk
of fixing Easter which would make potato planting
easier. No-one now uses their bare arse to test
the soil's warmth. Mine is pricked by sea holly
as I squat behind bushes, see cubs in the clearing.

Music & Movement

We're in our knickers, hungry as always.
Some of us are vestless but it's no disgrace,

it's months before we'll learn to be mortified
by nipples. After marching, we're divided:

tree-girls, static, arms aloft, and wind-boys
who career – hurricanes, tornados – oblivious

to the radio. Branches spread high and wide,
we trees persist in our valiant waving despite

the idiot winds' rude buffetings which knock us
sideways. I am silver birch, arboreally furious,

white-trunked in spotless cotton interlock.
My fringe is an owl, my beetle brows a hawk,

all murderous attention as twig fingers stir
and test the unsuspecting mouse-flavoured air.

My legs, my legs are mighty. No callow gusts
will better me. Each copse, each wood, each forest

will roar when I am wind, every single tree.
When I get to be wind, I'll do it properly.

When we were shortlifers in The Bury

And here were the people somehow left behind,
who hadn't made it up to Wild Street's sumptuous
bathrooms and electricity, who lacked the push,
that sure vocabulary of rights, to get themselves

decanted before we arrived – our careless caravan
of bean bags, marijuana and home-brew kits –
allowed to occupy the voids pending demolition.
A lav on the landing was small price for the chance

to play house at a peppercorn behind the Coliseum,
where Dickens lingered in the old photographer's
yellow vulpine smile, in the three slim sisters'
identical chignons, in the pantomime-costumed

bell-hop who beat his wife. These left-behind –
box office, porters, messengers for the Inns –
past the time of employment, edged warily round
us gong-voiced incomers who knew nothing

of Brasso, of turn and turnabout, who echoed all hours
in the corridors, colonising the cubbyhole bathroom
with our profligate steam, the air with our rootless music,
mislaid the keys, were there and then were gone.

Socialist Activist Anna Lindhagen
shows Lenin the Barnangen Allotments, Malmö, spring 1917

Welcome, welcome, Ulyanov. Stand here for a moment and look
at the clean land, the neatness of the rows of leeks. How it lifts
the heart to see such strong backs bent to the joy of providing!

How is poor Nadya's goitre? Has she tried the benefits of a sauna?
Or dandelion leaves rubbed on? It's the iodine. Let me introduce
my friend Anna. Yes, we're the two Annas. Just look at those cats

stretched out on the pumpkin mound enjoying the sunshine.
They keep the mice down. Anna says there's enough to share
but just you try telling that to the man who's lost all his peas.

I wish you could stay to see the gathering and heaping of beans
and lettuces, the berries and the doughty carrots. There's nothing
but good here. Anna and I say it's truly a Society of Abundance.

You'll agree a plot of land is a uniting bond? What could be
more satisfying than to feed your family, go home with a bag
of just-dug potatoes, tender and white as babies' knees?

You have no children, do you? Nor I. Do you garden at all?
Of course, your work makes it difficult but it's surprising
what can be achieved in one season. Please, take some of Anna's jam!

A jar of pickles then? Look, Ulyanov, see the ingenious cage?
It keeps pigeons off the brassicas, the devils. Some shoot them.
Must you go? You've not seen our root clamps or the compost heaps.

*n.b. Lenin's view was that 'to poke in the soil
is to prepare the ground for political laziness
in the class struggle. The workers should not
be occupied with gardening, they should rather
devote themselves to the proletarian revolution.'*

Ruby Wedding: what it's like

It's one of those wooden boxes on four legs.
On either side of the carrying handle, three tiers
of shallow trays fold out in steps, one half-tier adrift,

its struts come loose. I don't remember if
I bought it or was it a gift? Was it me picturing
myself head bent under lamplight or someone's

kind encouragement? Either way, it's full of stuff:
long skeins of faded silks from a brief passion
for embroidery, as much to do with the grace

of my hands rising and falling at the frame
as anything. Some are still banded and tidy,
some tangled beyond undoing from single

strands pulled out without first cutting
a length. Scraps of patterns, blue outlines
of monograms, floral posies, wrap around

spools of silver thread from my mandala phase:
such aspirations, so little patience, aptitude.
There are left-over patches from the time

of the Great Quilt. Sequins languish, untroubled
by needles trailing threads from name tags,
from taking up. A limp card bears press studs,

nested snug, male into female, waiting.
Another card is sewn with rows of metal hooks,
no eyes, for which you have to make your own

connecting loops by sewing over and over
your finger tip. Binding tape and jaunty rick-
rack braid acquired from my mother snag

in scissors long dull enough for children.
These buttons cut from the inside seams
of jackets or in neat envelopes or pearly,

saved from matinee coats, are tiny triggers.
Most ambitious of all, the intractable zips
and pocket linings: I conceded. It's like that.

Charles Boff's Comprehensive Guide

Inside, on cheap paper, a man with a pipe lifts
a barrow's handles and prepares to trundle it
past careful rows incised in wood: cabbage,
spuds, all cross-hatched and noble under
a half circle of sun and its rays, reprinted
in 1946 by Odhams, Long Acre, London WC2.

The very same press torched for its land value,
where we made a temporary garden.

Such orderly woodcuts, clean drawings
of dibbers, hoes, step-by-step instructions
for bastard trenching, how to use a trowel
and, in each, the lower part of a man's legs
clad in sturdy shoes and turn-ups as he looks
for first signs and accepts there is no cure.

Revelations

There's a vertical track in the cushiony flesh of my left lobe,
where a looked-after child on my lap caught and dragged,
not meaning to, a gold hoop to rest deep down. For months
I was lop-sided, until I summoned up the nerve to ease the ring
from its softly bedded place and leave my ears forever naked.

All my scars are ridiculous: negligible traces of mishaps,
like the sickle on my index finger memorialising the waste
of a whole block of cheese, at a time when it mattered,
the slipped knife having conjured such a startling amount
of blood; or the indentation, exquisitely neat and round,

bored in my left knee from when I misjudged a jump
over the garden rake I'd convinced my cousin could do
for a skipping rope; or the silver thread in the cross-hatch
on my right hand from the time I missed a step in the dark
of a poetry cellar and fell on a glass I hadn't had a sip from,

painlessly severing the tendon which operates the thumb.
It was fished down with something like a crochet hook
and reattached as though I was a pot doll whose rubber bands
had perished. I imagine there's a scar from the cut when I had
no push at all left in me but that's private and even I can't see it.

Taxonomy

The Architects and Lecturers have views
on rotavators, chemicals and committees.
They make successful funding bids for loos
that compost, organise muck deliveries
from local stables. They plant Florence
fennel, blue potatoes, then disappear
all summer to eat ratatouille in Provence,
handing their watering cans to a neighbour

but not to one of the ex-Sparks or Chippies,
Clerks or former Military who won't be told
what to do. They grow green gooseberries,
onions and cauliflowers. The very old
dig in relegated suits. They like a bonfire,
Bordeaux Mixture. They clean their tools
and forge a kinship with the Hippy via
a shared contempt for other people's rules.

The Hippy does exactly as he pleases, even
lives on his plot in a cleverly accoutred shed.
Surprisingly touchy for a Buddhist and vegan,
he bangs on and on about how he should be Head
or, at very least, Treasurer of the Association.
He excels at fruits, soft, stoned and pome,
gives tips on lunar planting and the application
of horn manure to the Capable Women known

for their willingness. They keep TCP to hand,
bring along brownies, wet wipes, milk for tea
and always share but sub in cheap own-brand
for the Choco Leibniz if they begin to feel... See
how, being Capable, one of them will always end up
as Hon Sec? They like authentic trugs, raised beds,
tiger tomatoes, purple spouting broccoli, a clean cup.
They've strong thighs from crouching and level heads.

No-one likes slugs or pigeons or that Malcom
from Leisure Services who promises swift action
on old carpet but only ever issues rote random
warnings about inadequate or patchy cultivation
or the keeping on site of disturbing cockerels
or the banned-on-pain-of-eviction hoses that snake,
not even half-concealed to the thirsty squash hills
from the standpipes. Everybody likes cake.

Covent Garden's garden

Now it's a blunt blind pile
of nothing-to-do-with-you,
something between Lubyanka
and the Great Pyramid at Giza,

but for two blue summers
it was our bowl of worms
where brick-born babies
aired rash and fat knees, toes
curling to the thrill of grass

and flushed children,
unlatched by clotted phlox,
Sweet William and sweetpeas,
filched unfeasibly sweet peas,
dangled from the bridge to tease
frilled axolotls with the pale gape
of throttled snapdragons.

Our hopeless defiance in Nelly Moser,
Scarlet Emperor, pursey lupins,
where caterpillars ruminated on
the costliest lettuces in London.

What I learnt behind bars

The Manvers Arms

I never saw the exotic dancer's snake,
being deemed too green for the hurly-burly
of the public bar and consigned upstairs
to the lounge, to ferry steaks au poivre
and cherries jubilee from the echoing kitchen
where a solitary boy in whites dropped
plastic sachets into water at a rolling boil
and gave up trying before he'd even started.

To a woman, the lady diners despised me
in my pink satin hot pants with the butterfly
appliqué. They were right. It wasn't a uniform,
nobody made me wear them but I had the legs.

The Flying Horse

I was filling in the rest of that last summer
when those Aussie lads we'd met
on the Piazzale Michelangelo
during the earth tremor
took us at our word,
hopped over to England and popped by.

It was several years until I came to see
that when the tidy men in the intimate bar

by the door had sighed I was lucky,
it hadn't been on account of my fabulous tan
or hair so straight it didn't need ironing

but because of those ragamuffin boys
who swept in and swept me up
in their loud glory, lighting every corner
with their shameless brio.

The Dover Castle

A solicitor called Christian owned the Dover Castle
and lived above with his largely incidental wife
who rose at six to make miniature shepherd's pies.

He had another round the corner but, it was agreed,
the Castle was the classier. By noon it was full
of doctors and the BBC drinking vodka and tonic.

On hot days he'd turn off the pumps and offer
only continental bottled beers to quench the thirst
of consultants, commissioning editors and engineers

sweating in the mews. If we had cucumbers,
he'd make up a jug of Pimms. In the afternoons
we bottled up, counted pennies from the machines

and American Annie whose husband was on the rigs
would explain how heroin was good for colds
but cocaine was a safer everyday choice

and Mitti would rail against the gracelessness
of English men. Of an evening it was quiet,
just regulars: a psychiatrist from Harley Street,

who specialised in Catholic guilt, drank
until he liquefied, and the man in the stetson
practiced being inscrutable over Jack Daniels.

Tipster Laurie, fresh from the courses, in thrall
to hard-hearted Mitti, could be coaxed into sending
a taxi for ice-cream as the dullness wore on,

soaked in scotches drawn from six optics, all filled
from the big bargain bottle. When David Warner,
in his Morgan years, sat on the step, head in hands,

I offered him the solace of the poster for his Hamlet
which had graced my teenage wall and agreed
that neither of us should be here. A man who said

he'd designed the packaging for Winalot invited me
to late supper at the Hard Rock Café and I went.
It seemed starry but really it was just sticky carpet work.

The Fancy

Those parakeets, they'd talk, especially the solitary males.
Let out to flit around the room, they'd settle on pelmets.
We'd bat them down with a copy of Woman's Realm.
Forget a window and they'd be off, leaving us to imagine them
harassed by duller local birds. No longer. In bullish flocks
they fly all along the Thames, right up to Hyde Park and beyond.
They escaped from the Twickenham set of *The African Queen*
or Jimi released two, Peace and Love, on Carnaby Street.

Nowadays, chickens are the bird of choice, some for The Fancy
but mostly for the upmanship of dirty eggs. Buff Orpingtons,
Scots Dumpies, manky rescue chooks and five-toed Turkish Sultans
scratch in back gardens, on allotments, circled by red mite and foxes.

Living in Seven Dials, I know it's not feasible, even with a patio,
but I've always wanted a peacock. I do admire the way they scream.

Cold Spell

From fifty yards away, the smell of the mimosa,
warm marzipan, crept over on a sharp wind.

We'd walked right under the old tree, taking
the back path to see if snow had browned

its yellow fuzz, if it had weathered the freeze,
but it was only once we were past Neptune

and his mermaids draped in sheets of ice
like frosted dreads which, from a distance

I'd thought some tall and tender plant swathed
in horticultural fleece, only across the grass,

clear except for stubborn heaps of yesterday's
snowmen, that the smell caught up with us,

seductive and insinuating as a memory
of something that has never really been.

The Ballad of St Giles Central

aka Legoland

Say, have you been to Legoland
and seen its mighty blocks
that thrust above our old St Giles
like multi-coloured cocks?

St Giles, that sanctuary of the poor,
in holy terror cowers
under the brash and braying roar
of Renzo Piano's towers.

Legoland, oh Legoland,
that monument to pride,
where the poor are kept in the shadows,
the rich on the sunny side.

St Giles, where poets' babes were blessed,
where Tyburn jigsters stopped
and all their many sins confessed
before they faced the drop,

is bullied by the ballyhoo
of Renzo's crass erection,
which turns an ancient high street to
a wind-blown intersection.

Legoland, oh Legoland,
that monument to graft,
where the rich live close to heaven's door
and the poor by the air-con shaft.

We pray to the gods of just desserts
that plague pits will crack wide,
and Giles's buzzmen, lepers and tarts
will swarm from every side,

that the rookery will rise once more
and topple Piano's piles –
then only honest thieves and whores
will dance in old St Giles.

Legoland, oh Legoland,
that monument to money,
where the poor endure, endure, endure
and the rich live on milk and honey.

Going to the Algerian Coffee Store: 500g Esotico

After the bin lorry has exhausted its beautifully modulated warnings,
after the glass lorry has shifted shingle, I step out into West Street

and the dog-end of last night, where a sweeper leans on his cart
and chats with his own country and a man with his trousers down

round his knees hobbles past, trailing a sleeping bag over his arm
like a negligent debutante with her stole. The pavements are tacky,

no loitering snappers, no witless number plates outside The Ivy yet,
just yellow drums of spent oil and bags of yesterday's fancy breads

awaiting their special collections under the heritage lamppost.
In what passes for peace, helicopters and gulls are still roosting

as I skirt the grim lieutenants outside Le Beaujolais, their hybrid engine
purring as they wait for lowly envoys on stolen bikes. My age exactly,

The Mousetrap sleeps the sleep of the utterly justified.

Or, I leave
by the front onto Earlham Street, its hat stall, cinnamon and falafel fug,

risk an erratic rickshaw bike's right turn, cross the Circus, passing
the latest sensation at The Palace, into Soho's loud and narrow scuzz

of £12 haircuts, tattooists, Aladdin, leather masks, the endless churn
of fit outs. And all the boys, the visitors, the louche remains of glory days

drink coffee on Old Compton Street, study each other side-eyed across
the blue recycling bags and natty dogs. The choice of pastries is infinite.

The Consultant Placemaker does Seven Dials

The Consultant Placemaker, a snazzy humdinger of a man
made of smoke, has come to tell us how to make our place

'a place'. He tells us history from the fourteenth century on.
He doesn't know, so doesn't speak about the rescued brace

of hooves from the magnificent horses rearing over
Odhams Press that ended up in Violet's fireplace.

He's never heard the invisible flock of sparrows above Nike.
Though he has no memories he's got a scheme, a database,

a Powerpoint presentation of 'quiet ways' which could
be made more profitable. He hasn't heard how Grace

and Mickey and the gang would tip the barrels of eels
to watch them thrash and slide down Lollipop Hill, chase

them down drainholes then run for their skinny lives.
The Consultant Placemaker talks on to make the case

for 'gateways to be more clearly signalled'. He doesn't know
the old girls' double names, Josie-Ryan-Josie-Doe-as-was, wastes

air concocting high street and pop-up village green equivalence,
says 'bunting creates character'. (I want to stab his shiny shiny face.)

The Consultant Placemaker has a lot of nerve for one who's never
bought nails from Freddie Collins's or climbed each stone staircase

of Wild Street to deliver news of money changing hands again.
But you have to hand it to him, he knows the marketplace.

Remedies against Enemies

Directly the petals have fallen, spray
by means of a syringe with arsenate
of lead, tar oil, slaked sulphur flowers.
codlin moth powdery mildew coral spot
When leaves are as large as a shilling,
dab liberally with a stiff brush dipped
in quassia solution, calomel or nicotine.
black knot disease apple sawfly cluster cup
On some sunless day or calm evening,
take up your special puffing device
and dust with soot or hellebore powder.
onion smut potato wart scale halo blight
In a disastrous year, put on old clothes,
gloves, a cap well down over the eyes.
Search for the entrance, pour in paraffin.
gall weevils rabbits flea beetle thrip
Drop in a lump of potassium cyanide,
walnut-sized, then, carefully, some water.
Seal with turf. Retire without loss of time.
eelworm cutworm leatherjackets scab
Enquire at the local Police Station
or dig flaked naphthalene into the ground.
Nip off affected tips. Send in the chickens.

The ironmonger's a vintage clothes shop now

There's only one other place this shape in England,
somewhere up North but I've forgotten its name,
this star, this timepiece, this little Paris that fell
to rookery then rose again, for now, so smart
even the rats keep a low profile. Not like that time
Freddie Collins (that's Fred Jnr, not young Freddie,
who didn't go into the business, not Fred Senior
at whose funeral we sang *Jerusalem* loud enough
to lift the roof off St Giles and, of course, not old FW,
sole inventor of elastic glue), unable to dispatch one
with a hammer, put it in a galvanised pail of water
where it scrabbled at the lid until it drowned.

Atomic Strip

Long ago and far away, well Maiden Lane until the 1970s,
there was a shop so confident it sold just the one thing,
its discrete window piled with flat brown boxes of coils,
shiny copper draft-excluder strips, all folded lengthways
to fit round doors, tapped on with dainty pins to spring
into gaps when wood shrinks from age or shifting ground.

When our front door rotted and was replaced, I realised,
too late, we'd never hear that mighty hum again,
that kazoo resonance along the hall and up the stairs,
when a big wind blew from exactly the right direction.

A Visit to the Master of Space and Light

It being neither wet nor dirty, I take myself to Lincoln's Inn Fields
and the complicated houses of Sir John Soane.

He knew how to let in light, funnel it
                                        through apertures,
                              domes or canopies and grilles, right down to
the Sepulchral Chamber and china pantry;

how to illuminate stuff – sarcophagi, casts, acanthus bosses, crocodiles, brass taps;

how to handle shadow – those yellow panes that mimic the fall
                                      of Mediterranean sunshine upon
the lovely buttocks of an Apollo Belvedere.

Quick footsteps on the stairs past Shakespeare's niche
could be applause for the sheer quantity of cartouches and fire-dogs,

so much,
        there is nowhere
                        to sit,
                              teasels on every reverend chair.

Soane's mild smile must belie insufferable drive.
Lampooning the Gothick, he interred: the family dog
in the lightwell out back,

in a monument
among ruins made from offcuts
from the Palace of Westminster.
Alas Poor Fanny;

his beloved Eliza
in a tomb which
would become
the template for
the telephone box   (She wrote, *John out of town… had a dance*).

And here's the thing – I think we share something, Sir John and I.

Not that I could build the Bank of England.
I can barely prise the plastic bung from a piggybank
and most of the stuff in my house
isn't actually mine.

But we're both listy, both suckers
for an accumulation of resonant fragments, cunning references,
a succession of those fanciful effects which constitute the poetry
of architecture and vice versa,
created by a coloured glow through
hidden skylights, more than one hundred mirrors.

ACKNOWLEDGEMENTS

Thank you to the editors who published some of these poems, or versions of them, in *And Other Poems, The Fenland Reed, The Morning Star, Poem, South Bank Poetry, The Stare's Nest* and *Ver Poetry Competition Anthology*.

My heartfelt thanks also go to Mimi Khalvati, Matthew Caley, Ann and Peter Sansom and Richard Price and to the talented and generous poets who gather round them for their insight, encouragement and friendship.

And I salute the stubborn and gloriously 'unreasonable' campaigners of The Seven Dials Trust and the Covent Garden Community Association, who never give up.

ABOUT THE POET

Kathy was born in Nottingham, in the shadow of Player's cigarette factory but has spent her adult life in London, the last 40 or so years in Covent Garden: specifically in Seven Dials.

She has had a rag-bag career in social work, community activism, arts television and artist development and now works on community-led public realm projects.

Her first pamphlet, *Goose Fair Night*, was published by the Emma Press in 2016 and her work has been widely published in magazines, on-line and in anthologies.

www.kathypimlott.co.uk
@kathy_pimlott